INTERFA

THE BOOK AND CD   TH

POLAR LANDS

TWO CAN™

PRINCETON ■ LONDON

www.two-canpublishing.com

Published in the United States and Canada by
Two-Can Publishing LLC, 234 Nassau Street, Princeton, NJ 08542

© 2001, 1998 Two-Can Publishing

CD
Creative Director: Jason Page
Programming Director: Brett Cropley
Art Director: Sarah Evans
Senior Designer: James Evans
Sub Editor: Jo Keane
Consultant: Graham Peacock
Illustrators: James Jarvis, Carlo Tartaglia,
Jeffrey Lewis, Nick Ward
Production Director: Lorraine Estelle
Project Manager: Joya Bart-Plange

Book
Creative Director: Jason Page
Editor: Jo Keane
Author: Monica Byles
Consultant: Graham Peacock
Designer: Michele Egar
Production Director: Lorraine Estelle
Project Manager: Joya Bart-Plange

Created by
act-two
346 Old Street, London EC1V 9RB

ISBN 1-58728-452-9

1 2 3 4 5 6 7 8 9 10 02 01

Photograph Credits: front cover: Getty Images
Ardea Ltd: p7, p12, p15, p16, p17t, p19b; Bruce Coleman: p6, p18, p23, p25;
NHPA: p8, p9, p17b, p26; Survival Anglia: p11, p14t, p19t, p24; B & C Alexander: p14b, p20, p27
All illustrations by Francis Mosley

Printed in Hong Kong by Wing King Tong

INTERFACT

THE BOOK AND CD — THAT WORK TOGETHER

INTERFACT will have you hooked in minutes –
and that's a fact!

🔵 **The disk is packed with interactive activities, puzzles, quizzes, and games that are fun to do and packed with interesting facts.**

Build an interactive food web and learn what different polar creatures eat.

Build the food web by dragging the icons into position with your mouse

Sea life

Icebergs are not the only things you will find in the polar oceans. The water is cold but it is teeming with life. As well as the creatures that live in the sea, many other animals take to the water in search of food. These include polar bears, penguins and seals.

In the Antarctic, currents from warmer seas encourage many varieties of colourful lifeforms. Bright-orange sea spiders, delicate anemones, fronds of primitive weeds, worms and other strange creatures are found on the sea floor.

Strange, ghostly fish live here too, such as the pole ice fish or the transparent deep-sea angler. These fish live in deep water. Very little light filters through to the depths so these creatures have no need for bright colouring.

AN ARCTIC FEAST

Sperm whales are toothed whales. They eat fish and squid.

Seals also feed on fish and squid.

Some types of fish are **herbivores**. Others are carnivores and eat krill and other fish.

Plankton are microscopic organisms. Some plankton are tiny plants, others are microscopic animals.

Krill are small sea creatures that feed on plankton.

◄ Krill are tiny crustaceans, similar to shrimps. Some countries have begun fishing krill to use as human food. This threatens the creatures of the polar lands that rely on krill as a food source.

...feed on krill ... whales which a series of bony plates in their mouths which helps them to filter out the krill from the water.

DISK LINK
Build your own interactive food webs and learn what's on the menu to the polar regions in Food For Thought.

▲ A killer whale breaching. Killer whales are in fact members of the dolphin family. They can swim at 65km/h. They live in all oceans but prefer the colder waters around the polar lands.

◄ This giant sea spider has 10 legs and lives on the ocean floor near Antarctica. The bodies of most sea spiders are so small that some of their food has to be digested in their legs.

Read about the fascinating creatures that live in the polar oceans.

🔵 **Open the book and discover more fascinating information highlighted with lots of full-color illustrations and photographs.**

🔵 To get the most out of **INTERFACT**, use the book and disk together. Look out for the special signs, called Disk Links and Bookmarks. To find out more, turn to page 43.

23

BOOKMARK

DISK LINK
Delve deeper into the history of the poles and take a trip in the Time Machine.

Once you've launched **INTERFACT**, you'll never look back.

LOAD UP!
Go to **page 40** to find out how to load your disk and click into action.

HELP SCREEN

Learn how to use the disk in no time at all.

Welcome to the

INTERFACT

disk on Polar Lands

To have a look at all the different things on the disk, simply click the arrow keys with your mouse.

As you do this, you'll see a description of each activity in the reading box.

Click on the picture at the top of the screen to select the activity you want to investigate.

Get to grips with the controls and find out how to use:

- arrow keys
- text boxes
- "hot" words

FOOD FOR THOUGHT

Create your own polar food web on screen!

Build an interactive food web for the Arctic or the Antarctic. Use your mouse to drag the animals and plants around the screen, and see if you can figure out who eats what.

CHILL OUT

It's time to put your knowledge of polar lingo to the test.

A T   This keeps seals and whales warm

BLU---R

This little penguin is stranded on a melting iceberg, and it's up to you to rescue him. Keep him from falling into the icy waters by figuring out a mystery polar word before time runs out.

SNOWBALL FIGHT

The polar lands quiz. It's a battle of brains – and snowballs!

Find out how much you know with this quiz on the polar lands. Each correct answer earns you snowballs to throw at your opponent. Play against a friend or challenge the computer!

POLES APART

What's the difference between the Arctic and the Antarctic?

Try to match up each of the interactive icons on the screen with the correct polar landscape. Discover the important differences between the two polar lands.

EXPLORE THE POLAR LANDS

Take a look at an interactive polar landscape.

Use your mouse to get a close-up look at the Arctic and the Antarctic. Discover all you need to know about the animals and plants that survive in this incredible environment.

ALL THE ANSWERS

Introducing Sidney the Seal and Alberta the Albatross.

Sidney the Seal is full of questions about the polar lands – just like you! Pick a question you want Sid to ask then click on Alberta the Albatross to find out the answer.

TIME MACHINE

Get the lowdown on the history of the polar lands.

In 1959, 12 countries signed the Antarctic Treaty. According to the treaty, Antarctica may only be used for peaceful purposes and scientists must share all their discoveries.

Go on a journey of discovery and travel back in time. Learn about the fascinating history of the polar lands, from prehistoric times right up to the present day.

What's in the book

*All words in the text that appear in **bold** can be found in the glossary*

Looking at the poles

Few places in the world are as harsh and barren as the areas surrounding the North and South poles. And few places are as beautiful. For much of the year, both areas are freezing cold, with thick snow and ice on the ground and fierce winds. As it grows colder, even the seas freeze.

It is hard to imagine that anything could survive in such an extreme climate. But many plants, animals, and people have made this frozen habitat their home.

In the summer months – May to July at the North Pole and November to January at the South Pole – the sun shines even at midnight. But in winter, the poles remain almost permanently dark.

In the short Arctic summers, the snow and ice melt, leaving pools of **meltwater** on the ground. The land bursts into life. Flowers and plants grow, and the air is filled with insects. Animals mate and find safe places to raise their young.

▶ Plants in the polar lands spend most of the year under snow. Their seeds are hardy and do not **germinate** until the short summer when conditions are exactly right for growth.

DISK LINK
What's the difference between the Arctic and the Antarctic? Find out in Poles Apart!

▼ A large **iceberg** floats in the sea during the Antarctic summer. It is evening, but at this time of year the sky is never very dark.

Where in the world?

The poles are at the top and bottom of the earth. The sun's rays strike the earth at a lower angle at the poles. As a result, they receive less of the sun's warmth than anywhere else. This is why the polar lands are the coldest places in the world.

The North Pole lies in the middle of a frozen sea called the Arctic Ocean. It is surrounded by Northern Europe, Russia, and North America. The most northerly point where trees will grow, called the **tree line,** is about 1,430 miles (2,300 km) from the North Pole. Between the tree line and the **icecap** are regions of rough terrain called **tundra**. The ground is always frozen beneath the tundra, even in the summer. This layer of frozen earth is called **permafrost**.

The continent of Antarctica lies around the South Pole. It is permanently covered in a thick shield of ice. Snow and ice lie deeper here than anywhere else on earth.

HISTORY OF THE POLES

● **150 to 170 million years ago**
The poles are not frozen. The South Pole probably lies over low ground and the North Pole over the sea.

● **60 to 70 million years ago**
Shifts in the earth's **plates** cause the polar lands to move to the positions where they are now. They begin to cool.

● **5 to 6 million years ago**
Changes in the climate and in the heat received from the sun bring new conditions of snow and ice.

NORTH POLE FACTS

● The Arctic Ocean is surrounded by land. Consequently, currents from warmer seas cannot reach it and raise the temperature.

● The ancient Greeks named the Arctic after a group of stars known as *Arktos,* meaning the Great Bear.

● In 1909, Robert Peary and Matthew Henson became the first explorers to reach the North Pole.

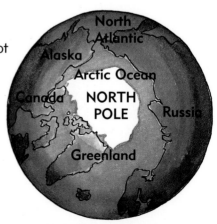

North Atlantic
Alaska
Arctic Ocean
Canada
NORTH POLE
Russia
Greenland

The polar lands were not always so cold. Fossils of trees, plants, and animals in Antarctica show that it once had a much warmer climate. Over millions of years, the Earth's land masses have moved, and the temperature has changed. This has brought about the freezing conditions at the poles today.

▲ A herd of caribou makes its annual journey to the rich feeding grounds of the Arctic tundra.

DISK LINK
Delve deeper into the history of the poles and take a trip in the Time Machine.

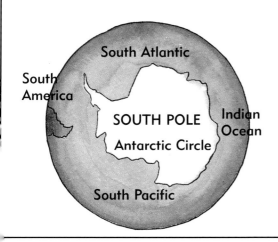

South Atlantic

South America

SOUTH POLE

Antarctic Circle

Indian Ocean

South Pacific

SOUTH POLE FACTS

● About 70 percent of the world's fresh water is stored in the Antarctic icecap.

● The inland plateau of Antartica can be called a desert because it receives about 2 inches (5 cm) of snow per year.

● In 1911, the Norwegian explorer Roald Amundsen beat Britain's Robert Scott to the South Pole by one month.

Frozen features

A quarter of the world's oceans and seas are affected by ice every year. Around the poles, the sea actually freezes. Icebergs from polar regions also float across other oceans. One iceberg from Antarctica almost reached Rio de Janeiro in Brazil – a journey of 3,400 miles (5,500 km).

Ice covers most of the land around the South Pole. This blanket of ice forms **glaciers** that spread across the continent until they reach the sea. Sometimes the long, icy fingers of the glacier break, and huge chunks of ice fall into the ocean. This is how icebergs are formed.

◀ The Paradise Bay Glacier is in Antarctica. Sections break off from its craggy cliffs and plummet into the clear waters below to form icebergs.

In 1912, an ocean liner called the *Titanic* collided with an iceberg in the North Atlantic Ocean. The ship sank with the loss of 1,517 lives. Ever since the disaster, the International Ice Patrol has monitored icebergs and alerted ships to danger.

Icebergs are made from frozen fresh water, but the salty ocean around the poles also freezes. Freezing reaches a peak during the months of February and March, when there is about 4.6 million square miles (12 million km^2) of sea ice in the Arctic Ocean and 1 million square miles (3 million km^2) off Antarctica.

As the sea freezes, a greasy film appears to cover the surface of the water. Wisps of smoky vapor rise from the surface and as the seawater turns to ice, salt is pushed above the surface in beautiful crystals called **ice flowers**.

DIFFERENT KINDS OF ICE

● **Tabular** icebergs have flat tops. Some are several miles or kilometers long, and scientists sometimes use them as convenient research bases.

● Pieces of frozen seawater are called **floes**. When a lot of floes gather, they form pack ice. The wind and ocean currents push the pack ice around the polar seas.

● The ice at the outer edges of a glacier is usually very dense and very old. The ice in some glaciers was formed many thousands of years ago.

● Large pieces of ice break off from icebergs to form floating chunks known as **bergy bits**. Smaller fragments of floating ice are known as **growlers**.

Animal life

Despite the bleakness of the polar lands, many animals live here. Some remain all year round, while others are only summer visitors.

The only permanent residents on the Antarctic mainland are insects. Penguins and seals make their homes on the ice at the edge of the ocean, and the waters of Antarctica are teeming with life.

An enormous variety of animals live in the Arctic, from tiny shrews to huge polar bears. Native species are well adapted to make good use of the short summer and to protect themselves against the long, cold winter.

Many polar animals are larger than similar creatures in warmer climates. They have short legs, long hair, and a dense undercoat. Their tails are short, and the pads on their feet are furry.

▲ The stoat grows a white **pelt** during the winter for **camouflage**. This helps it to hunt and avoid predators.

▼ Polar bear cubs are born in pairs and stay with their mother for up to two years. They live as long as 33 years in the wild.

▶ Seals come in many shapes and sizes, but they all are superbly adapted to life in the water. Their sleek, torpedo-like shape and their strong flippers help them move easily through the water. Seals' bodies are covered in a thick layer of **blubber** that protects their internal organs from the cold. This blubber also provides seals with energy. Seals can live off their reserves of blubber when food is scarce.

Life in the Arctic is a delicate balancing act. The number of plants affects the number of small animals, which affects the number of **carnivores**. The carnivores eat the small animals – which, in turn, affects the number of plants!

DISK LINK
Some words on this page will help you to save the penguin when you play Chill Out!

◀ A pack of wolves follows its leader into the tree line. A pack is a family group with about eight members. Most wolves have gray fur, but the fur of Arctic wolves is usually white. Their coats are long and thick to help keep them warm. A wolf can see and smell its prey over a mile (1.6 km) away. Wolves can eat up to 20 pounds (9 kg) of food at one time, but they also can go without eating for two weeks or longer.

Birdland

Winter in the polar lands is too cold for most birds, but many species arrive during the summer. The Arctic tern has the longest journey of any polar visitor. It flies from summer at one pole to summer at the other, covering 18,600 miles (30,000 km) every year. Other birds include ducks such as widgeons, eiders, and teals as well as geese, larks, and pipits.

On the ground lie pools of melted ice and snow, where millions of mosquitoes and other insects flourish. The humming air is a feast for birds!

Some birds spend the winter on the **subarctic** wastes of the tundra. They feed on roots and berries under the snow or hunt other birds, small mammals, or insects. The ptarmigan, snowy owl, raven, and Arctic redpoll live close to the tree line in this region.

Unlike other birds, many penguins spend their entire lives in the Antarctic. They are protected from the cold by a thick layer of blubber and waterproof feathers. Some penguins can dive as deep as 850 feet (260 m) under the water in search of fish.

King penguins spend up to a month at sea searching for food to feed their chicks. Back on shore, the penguins huddle for warmth. The cold penguins from the edge of the group trade places with the warmer birds in the center every few minutes.

Young king penguins soon grow into enormous, brown, fluffy chicks. Some chicks weigh up to 26 pounds (12 kg)!

DISK LINK
How many different kinds of penguins live in Antarctica? Find out when you EXPLORE THE POLAR LANDS.

◀ At about 4 feet (1.2 m) tall and 100 pounds (45 kg), the emperor penguin is the largest penguin. The male **incubates** the egg by using his feet to hold it against his body. He goes without food for as long as two months while caring for the chick.

▲ A black-browed albatross flies over the southern ocean. It has long, thin wings that help it glide through the air.

▼ Puffins live around the Arctic Circle and nest among the rocky cliffs on the Pacific coasts of Alaska and Russia.

Sea life

There's more than icebergs in the polar oceans. The water is cold, but it teems with life. In addition to the sea's permanent residents, many other animals take to the water in search of food. These include polar bears, penguins, and seals.

In the Antarctic, currents from warmer seas nourish many varieties of colorful lifeforms. Bright-orange sea spiders, delicate anemones, fronds of primitive seaweeds, worms, and other strange creatures live on the sea floor.

Other Antarctic Ocean inhabitants are strange, ghostly fish, such as the pale ice fish and the transparent deep-sea anglerfish. These fish live in deep water. Very little light reaches such depths, so these creatures have no need for bright coloring.

A POLAR FEAST

Sperm whales are **toothed whales**. They eat fish and squid.

Seals also feed on fish and squid.

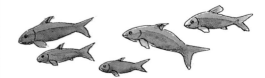

Some types of fish are seaweed-eating **herbivores**. Others are carnivores and eat krill and other fish.

Plankton is made up of microscopic organisms. Some of the plankton consists of algae, and some of tiny animals.

Krill are small sea creatures that feed on plankton.

◀ Krill are tiny crustaceans similar to shrimps. Some countries have begun fishing for krill to use as human food. This threatens the polar creatures that rely on krill as a food source.

Some of these bizarre creatures have special organs in their bodies that produce light. This enables them to see in the dark depths near the seabed.

The largest marine animals, whales, also swim in the waters around the polar lands. Biggest of all is the blue whale, which grows up to 100 feet (30 m) long and weighs up to 150 short tons (135 metric tons). There are two groups of whales – toothed whales, which feed on fish and squid, and **baleen whales**, which feed on krill. Baleen whales have a series of bony plates in their mouths that they use to filter krill from the water.

DISK LINK
Build your own interactive food web to learn what's on the menu in the polar regions in Food For Thought.

▲ A killer whale **breaches**, or leaps from the water. They can swim at 25 miles (40 km) per hour. Killer whales are members of the dolphin family. They live in all oceans but prefer the colder polar waters.

◀ This giant sea spider has 10 legs and lives on the ocean floor near Antarctica. The bodies of most sea spiders are so small that some of their food has to be digested in their legs!

People of the poles

Antarctica has no native human inhabitants. The only people who live there are scientists who brave the region to carry out experiments.

People have lived in the Arctic, on the other hand, for thousands of years. Some still live as **nomads**, following the herds of animals that provide their livelihood. Today, however, a great number of the native peoples have made their homes in modern settlements.

The Inuit, or Eskimo as they are sometimes known, are the most widespread group of Arctic people.

▼ The Inuit still build igloos for use as overnight resting places on long hunting trips. Igloos are made from slabs of ice, cut to size and fitted together. The Inuit produce light inside the igloo by burning whale or seal oil in a small container. This also helps to keep the igloo warm inside.

DISK LINK
Want to ask a question about polar people? Click on Sidney the Seal in All The Answers!

Inuit live in North America and Russia. Some Inuit people still drive sledges pulled by dogs and wear clothes made from animal skins. But most prefer to ride over the icecap on snowmobiles and wear modern parkas, even though their traditional stitched skins are warmer.

The increased freedom granted to the people of Eastern European countries in the late 1980's means that Arctic people are now able to travel more freely than they could under the old laws. Today, the closely related Inuit tribes of Alaska and Russia are allowed to meet without regard to political boundaries.

In the future, the peoples of the north may find it easier to fish and hunt where the animals are and not where governments want them to live.

POLAR PEOPLE

● Viking explorers were the first Europeans to meet Inuit people.

● Inuit eat mostly fish and meat because few plants grow in the Arctic.

● More than 100,000 Inuit live in four countries along the Arctic coast.

▲ This picture shows an Inuit man wearing traditional boots, leggings, trousers, jacket, and mittens. These clothes are made from caribou, bear, or wolf skins. They are worn loose to trap warm air. The seams are tightly sewn to make the garments waterproof.

Watching the weather

Polar lands are particularly useful places to study the weather. **Meteorologists** monitor the poles with interest because conditions in the Arctic and Antarctic affect the climate all over the world. For example, when cold air from the poles meets warm air from tropical regions, it can change the weather where you live.

▼ If the polar icecaps were to melt because of global warming, many countries around the world would be flooded. Important cities, including those on the map below, could be lost beneath the waters.

THE EARTH'S ATMOSPHERE

ionosphere

stratosphere

troposphere

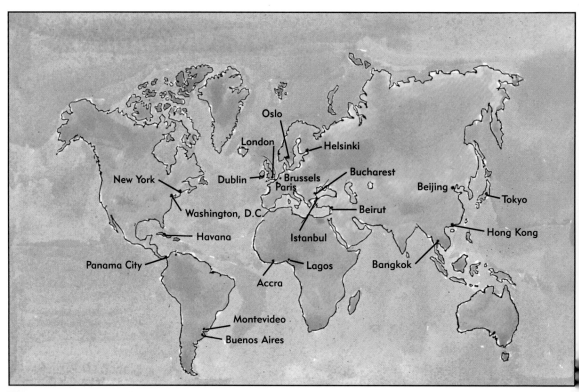

Scientists also are very concerned about the **ozone layer** above the poles. This is the layer of the earth's stratosphere that protects us from the sun's harmful ultraviolet rays. The ozone layer is being destroyed by chemicals such as chlorofluorocarbons (known as CFCs for short), which are used in some aerosol sprays, foam packaging, and refrigerators. Holes have appeared in the ozone layer above the poles.

Scientists at the poles investigate long-term changes in the earth's climate, such as global warming. By examining ice that formed hundreds or even thousands of years ago, they can discover what the temperature of the earth was like then and if it is changing.

▲ The aurora borealis, caused when solar particles contact the earth's magnetic field, is a beautiful sight near the North Pole. A similar display in the Antarctic is known as the aurora australis.

HOW YOU CAN HELP SAVE THE EARTH

● Stop using sprays that contain CFCs. These chemicals destroy the ozone layer. Look for alternatives, which are now easy to find in supermarkets. Most are labeled "Contains no chlorofluorocarbons."

● An average car powered by gasoline produces its own weight in carbon dioxide fumes every year. Carbon dioxide is one of the major greenhouse gases responsible for global warming. So, why not try to walk or ride your bicycle if you can, instead of traveling in a car?

Global warming is a potential ecological disaster. It is caused by **greenhouse gases** building up in the earth's atmosphere. These gases act as a blanket and trap more of the sun's heat around the earth. As a result, the temperature of the earth could rise.

At present, polar temperatures rise only to 50° F. (10° C) at the height of the summer. If the temperature in the polar lands were to rise by more than five percent at the poles, the ice would melt and sea levels across the world could rise drastically. Low-lying cities, such as London and New York, as well as whole countries like the Netherlands and Bangladesh, could be flooded. At these temperatures, many of the animals and plants in the polar regions would die out, too.

Exploiting the poles

The first outsiders to see the potential for making money at the poles arrived during the 1800's. They killed many whales for their meat and blubber, which was used in a variety of products from soap to oil. People trapped seals, particularly fur seals, for their attractive pelts. They killed penguins because oil from their bodies made good lamp oil.

Today, international agreements protect the creatures of the poles from hunters. A few animals are still killed each year for scientific purposes, and native peoples are also permitted to hunt a small number of animals.

However, the animals now face other dangers. Polar bears, for example, are scavengers and sometimes become dependent on scientific bases for scraps of food. They often visit garbage dumps, where they may eat unsuitable things or cut themselves. Some bears lose the desire to hunt altogether.

But it is not just the animals that are in danger. Some scientists fear that dust and grime from the refineries and other industries in the Arctic might make the ice dirty and darker.

This could make global warming worse and might lead to a dangerous increase in the earth's temperature. How? The

DISK LINK
Read this page carefully! It will help you earn the ammunition you'll need in the Snowball Fight.

POLAR RESOURCES

● Beneath the thick ice that covers 98 percent of Antarctica may lie valuable deposits of rubies and other minerals.

● Reserves of oil and natural gas lie under Alaska, Arctic Canada, and Siberia. More oil deposits are found off the coast of Greenland, on the Arctic shores of the North Atlantic, and in parts of the southern ocean.

● Oil spilled from a tanker accident in Alaska in 1989 caused the death of many birds and other animals.

◀ The white bones of dead whales remind us of the years when these creatures were hunted mercilessly. One type of baleen whale even became known as the "right whale" because it was so easy to catch.

▲ A polar bear forages among the litter of a settlement in northern Canada. It may be poisoned or injured, and it also poses a serious threat to local inhabitants.

glaring white surface of the icecap at each pole reflects some of the sun's energy back into space. This helps keep the temperature of the earth's atmosphere from increasing.

Dark colors, on the other hand, soak up the sun's warmth. (This is why wearing dark clothes in summer makes you feel hot, while light clothes keep you cool.) If large areas of the Arctic icecap get darker as a result of pollution, the effects on our environment could be disastrous!

Saving the poles

▲ This is a rookery of king penguins. These creatures have adapted well to the extreme cold of Antarctica, but they may not survive if the poles become warmer as a result of global warming.

It is important that people realize the value of the polar lands. Polar animals and plants will die if the temperature in these regions rises by even a small amount. What is more, if the poles were to melt, the impact on the rest of the world would be devastating.

Measures have been taken to establish the polar regions as places of special scientific interest rather than as lands to be exploited. The Antarctic Treaty, concerning the ownership of the South Pole's lands, has now been agreed to by most governments.

Even industry has taken steps to avoid further damage to these precious environments. Special ice roads have been built to prevent plants from being crushed under the wheels of heavy vehicles.

Similarly, oil and gas pipelines are raised above the ground like bridges. Despite the continuing encroachment on the polar lands, the caribou in the north may continue their migration in peace.

DISK LINK
Play Explore the Polar Lands and find out even more about our feathered friends, the penguins!

▶ These are the snow-crusted ridges of Greenland. The world would lose one of its great natural beauties if we allow the destruction of the polar icecaps.

Crow steals some daylight

For thousands of years, people have told stories about the world around them. Often, these stories try to explain something that people do not understand, like how the world began. The Inuit people who live in the polar lands of northern Canada tell this tale to explain where light comes from.

Long ago, in the northern lands where the Inuit live, there was no daylight. The people slept, hunted, cooked, ate, and played all in darkness. There was no light to tell the people when it was day and when it was night, so they all got up at different times. When they needed to see, they would light little seal-oil lamps that gave off a small glimmer of light,

scarcely enough to see by.

In one village lived a wise, old crow. He used to tell the Inuit people stories of the far-off lands that he had visited on his travels. One day, he told them about a distant land where there was light all

the time. The people of this land could see without using lamps or fires and could spot animals in the distance. This helped them to stay out of danger and to hunt for food more easily. The villagers were amazed at what the crow said and began to realize how difficult their lives were without light.

"When we go fishing," said one,

"we have to cut a hole in the ice and then shine a light into it to see if there are any fish there. The fish see the light and they are scared off. If it were light all the time, we would be able to see the fish before they saw us."

"And without light," said another, "we might walk straight into the arms of a polar bear before we even realize that it's there. If it were light all the time, we would be able to see them in the distance and keep away."

All the villagers begged the crow to go to the land of daylight and fetch them some light. At first the crow refused, because it was such a long journey. But the villagers had always been very good to him, so eventually he agreed.

It was a very long journey indeed and when, at last, the crow reached the lands where the sky was bright with daylight, he sank to the ground, exhausted. He found himself in a village not so very different from the one he had left. But in the middle of the village was a house from which daylight shone brightly.

"Aha!" thought the crow. "That is where the daylight comes from."

As he watched, a woman walked toward the house. The crow flew over to the door, shook off his skin, and turned himself into a speck of dust, which settled on the woman's dress as she went inside.

In the house, a great chief sat watching a baby playing on a fur rug. As the woman passed, she bent down and tickled the baby. She didn't notice the tiny speck of dust fall from her dress and into the little baby's ear. It was the crow of course!

The baby tugged at its ear, which tickled dreadfully, and began to cry, whereupon the chief and the woman leaped to their feet and began to fuss over it.

"Ask for some daylight," whispered the speck of dust.

So the baby cried for some daylight. The chief picked up a carved wooden box, placed it before the baby, and opened the lid. Inside were seven glowing balls of daylight. The chief took out one and gave it to the baby. The baby was so delighted with its new toy that all its tears were gone at once.

"Ask for a string to be tied to the ball," whispered the speck of dust in the little baby's ear.

And the baby began to cry for a string to be tied to the beautiful ball of daylight.

As soon as the chief had tied a string to the ball and given it to the baby, the speck of dust whispered in the baby's ear again.

"Move over to the doorway."

The baby crawled over to the doorway of the hut, trailing the ball of daylight on its string, and sat, framed by the arch, with daylight shining brightly all around.

Gradually the baby moved farther and farther out of the house, dangling the ball, right to the very spot where the crow had left his skin. Quick as a flash, the speck of dust fell out of the baby's ear, picked up the skin, and became a crow again. The crow snatched the string from the baby and flew off with the bright ball. All the villagers rushed out of their houses. They threw stones at the crow and tried to shoot him down with their bows and arrows. But the crow flew off toward his home much too fast for them.

At last, the crow came to the land of the Inuit. As he soared over village after village, he broke off a piece of daylight from the ball over each one that he passed and let it fall to the ground. Finally, after much traveling, he reached the village that he had set off from. Then he let go of the string, and all that was left of the ball of daylight fell to the ground and shattered into millions of tiny fragments. Shafts of light burst from the ground and streamed into all the houses. The villagers rushed toward the crow to thank him for his wonderful gift.

The crow told the villagers how he had stolen the light from the great chief in the south. He explained to them that he had not brought enough light for them to have daylight all the time. There was only enough light for half the year, and they would have to spend the other half of the year in darkness.

"But," the crow said wisely, "if I had brought enough daylight for it to be always light, you would have had as much trouble as you did when it was always dark!" But that's a story for another day.

True or false?

Which of these facts are true and which are false?
If you have read this book carefully, you will know the answers!

1. Summer falls between May and July at both poles.

2. No plants grow in the polar lands.

3. Millions of years ago, Antarctica had a much warmer climate.

4. The Arctic was named by the ancient Greeks after the constellation of the Plow.

5. Roald Amundsen was the first person to reach the South Pole.

6. The *Titanic* sank in 1912 after running into a whale.

7. Large fragments from the ice sheet are called bergy growlers.

8. The largest permanent residents on the Antarctic ice sheet are insects.

9. A male emperor penguin can go as long as two months without food.

10. Polar bear cubs are born two at a time.

11. Arctic people are mostly vegetarian.

12. A car running on gasoline releases its own weight in carbon dioxide fumes every year.

ANSWERS: 1.F 2.F 3.T 4.F 5.T 6.F 7.F 8.T 9.T 10.T 11.F 12.T

Glossary

Baleen whales have sheets of bony plates in their mouths. These allow them to filter krill out of the water.

Bergy bits are large, floating chunks of ice that are roughly the same size as an average house.

Blubber is the thick layer of fat on animals such as seals, walruses, penguins, and whales. Blubber helps to protect them against the cold. In the past, people used blubber to make goods such as soap and oil for household lighting.

Breaching is another term for leaping clear above the water.

Camouflage is used by animals to hide themselves in their surroundings. For example, the white winter coat of an Arctic fox makes the animal invisible against the snow. Camouflage helps to protect an animal from predators and also helps it to capture prey.

Carnivores are meat-eating animals.

Floes are pieces of frozen seawater. Some are a few yards or meters long, while others are 6 miles (10 km) in length!

Germination is the moment when plant seeds begin to sprout. They are roused from their dormant state by suitable conditions for growth.

Glacier is a river of ice that moves very slowly, pushed by new ice that forms on higher ground.

Greenhouse gases, such as carbon dioxide, collect in the earth's atmosphere. They trap heat rays from the sun and prevent them from bouncing back into outer space. Because of this, the earth's climate may be growing warmer.

Growlers are chunks of ice that are smaller than bergy bits. Growlers get their name because of the growling noise they make as they float in the sea.

Herbivores are plant-eating animals.

Iceberg is a large lump of ice that floats in the sea. Many icebergs are chunks of ice that have broken off glaciers. Usually, only 10 percent of an iceberg shows above the surface of the water.

Icecap is a name for the huge shield of ice that covers both the Arctic Ocean and Antarctica.

Ice flowers form when salt is pushed out of seawater as it freezes. The salt forms arrangements of beautiful crystals.

Ice sheet is another name for a continental glacier.

Incubation is the time between the laying of a bird's egg and its hatching.

Meltwater is the water that appears when ice and snow melt in summer. In some areas, meltwater can cause flooding.

Meteorologists study earth's atmosphere and weather. They pay particular attention to air moisture and temperature.

Nomads are people who do not have a settled home. Instead, they follow their herds of animals in search of fresh pasture. The Lapps of northern Scandinavia travel in this way, tending their reindeer.

Ozone layer prevents the sun's harmful ultraviolet rays from entering the earth's atmosphere. A hole in this layer is forming over each pole.

Pack ice is made up of pieces of frozen seawater called floes.

Pelt is the name for an animal skin.

Permafrost is an underground layer of soil that remains frozen all year, even during the polar summer.

Plates are huge sections of the earth's crust. These plates move slowly over hundreds of thousands of years. As the plates meet and their edges grind against each other, volcanoes erupt and earthquakes occur.

Subarctic describes the area south of the Arctic. Winter in the subarctic is very cold, but summer there is warmer than in the Arctic.

Tabular icebergs have a large, flat surface like that of a table.

Toothed whales have peglike teeth. They eat animals such as seals, squid, and fish.

Tree line is the farthest point to the north that trees can grow. North of the tree line, the climate is too harsh for trees.

Tundra is the belt of land between the Arctic ice sheet and the tree line. The word *tundra* comes from a Finnish word meaning barren land. Rough scrub is the only vegetation there, and the land is characterized by lakes, bogs, and streams.

Lab pages

Loading your INTERFACT disk

INTERFACT is easy to load. But, before you begin, quickly run through the checklist on the opposite page to ensure that your computer is ready to run the program.

Your INTERFACT CD-ROM will run on both PCs with Windows and on Apple Macs. To make sure that your computer meets the system requirements, check the list below.

SYSTEM REQUIREMENTS

PC/WINDOWS
- Pentium 100Mhz processor
- Windows 95 or 98 (or later)
- 16Mb RAM (24Mb recommended for Windows 98)
- VGA 256 color monitor
- SoundBlaster-compatible soundcard
- 1Mb graphics card
- Double-speed CD-ROM drive

APPLE MAC
- 68020 processor (PowerMac or G3/iMac recommended)
- System 7.0 (or later)
- 16Mb RAM
- Color monitor set to at least 480 x 640 pixels and 256 colors
- Double-speed CD-ROM drive

LOADING INSTRUCTIONS

You can run INTERFACT from the CD – you don't need to install it on your hard drive.

PC WITH WINDOWS 95 OR 98

The program should start automatically when you put the disk in the CD drive. If it does not, follow these instructions.

1. Put the disk in the CD drive
2. Open MY COMPUTER
3. Double-click on the CD drive icon
4. Double-click on the icon called POLAR

PC WITH WINDOWS 3.1 OR 3.11

1. Put the disk in the CD drive
2. Select RUN from the FILE menu in the PROGRAM MANAGER
3. Type D:\POLAR (Where D is the letter of your CD drive)
4. Press the RETURN key

APPLE MAC

1. Put the disk in the CD drive
2. Double-click on the INTERFACT icon
3. Double-click on the icon called POLAR

CHECKLIST

● Firstly, make sure that your computer and monitor meet the system requirements as set out on page 40.

● Ensure that your computer, monitor and CD-ROM drive are all switched on and working normally.

● It is important that you do not have any other applications, such as wordprocessors, running. Before starting INTERFACT quit all other applications.

● Make sure that any screen savers have been switched off.

● If you are running INTERFACT on a PC with Windows 3.1 or 3.11, make sure that you type in the correct instructions when loading the disk, using a colon (:) not a semi-colon (;) and a back slash (\) not a forward slash (/). Also, do not use any other punctuation or put any spaces between letters.

How to use INTERFACT

INTERFACT is easy to use.
First find out how to load the program
(see page 40), then read these simple
instructions and dive in!

You will find that there are lots of different features to explore.
To select one, operate the controls on the right-hand side of the screen. You will see that the main area of the screen changes as you click on different features.

For example, this is what your screen will look like when you play Explore the Polar Lands – an interactive polar landscape you can visit. Once you've selected a feature, click on the main screen to start playing.

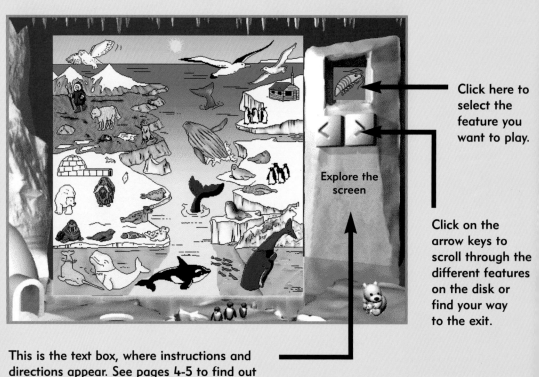

Explore the screen

Click here to select the feature you want to play.

Click on the arrow keys to scroll through the different features on the disk or find your way to the exit.

This is the text box, where instructions and directions appear. See pages 4-5 to find out what's on the disk.

DISK LINKS

When you read the book, you'll come across Disk Links. These show you where to find activities on the disk that relate to the page you are reading. Use the arrow keys to find the icon on screen that matches the one in the Disk Link.

DISK LINK
Spot the differences between the Antarctic and the Arctic. They're Poles Apart!

BOOKMARKS

As you explore the features on the disk, you'll bump into Bookmarks. These show you where to look in the book for more information about the topic on screen. Just turn to the page of the book shown in the Bookmark.

23

LAB PAGES

On pages 36 – 39, you'll find pages to photocopy. These are for making notes and recording any thoughts or ideas you may have as you read the book.

HOT DISK TIPS

- After you have chosen the feature you want to play, remember to move the cursor from the icon to the main screen before clicking the mouse again.

- If you don't know how to use one of the on-screen controls, simply touch it with your cursor. An explanation will pop up in the text box!

- Keep a close eye on the cursor. When it changes from an arrow ➔ to a hand, ☞ click your mouse and something will happen.

- Any words that appear on screen in blue and underlined are "hot." This means you can touch them with the cursor for more information.

- Explore the screen! There are secret hot spots and hidden surprises to find.

Troubleshooting

If you come across a problem loading or running the INTERFACT disk, you should find the solution here. If you still cannot solve your problem, call the helpline at 1-800-424-1280.

QUICK FIXES Run through these general checkpoints before consulting COMMON PROBLEMS (see opposite page).

QUICK FIXES

PC WITH WINDOWS 3.1 OR 3.11

1 Check that you have the minimum system requirements: 386/33Mhz, VGA color monitor, 4Mb of RAM.

2 Make sure you have typed in the correct instructions: a colon (:) not a semi-colon (;) and a back slash (\) not a forward slash (/). Also, do not put any spaces between letters or punctuation.

3 It is important that you do not have any other programs running. Before you start **INTERFACT**, hold down the Control key and press Escape. If you find that other programs are open, click on them with the mouse, then click the End Task key.

QUICK FIXES

PC WITH WINDOWS 95

1 Make sure you have typed in the correct instructions: a colon (:) not a semicolon (;) and a back slash(\) not a forward slash (/). Also, do not put any spaces between letters or punctuation.

2 It is important that you do not have any other programs running. Before you start **INTERFACT**, look at the task bar. If you find that other programs are open, click with the right mouse button and select Close from the pop-up menu.

MACINTOSH

1 Make sure that you have the minimum system requirements: 68020 processor, 640x480 color display, system 7.0 (or a later version), and 4Mb of RAM.

2 It is important that you do not have any other programs running. Before you start **INTERFACT**, click on the application menu in the top right-hand corner. Select each of the open applications and select Quit from the File menu.

COMMON PROBLEMS

 Symptom: Cannot load disk.
Problem: There is not enough space available on your hard disk.
Solution: Make more space available by deleting old applications and files you don't use until 6Mb of free space is available.

 Symptom: Disk will not run.
Problem: There is not enough memory available.
Solution: *Either* quit other open applications (see Quick Fixes) *or* increase your machine's RAM by adjusting the Virtual Memory.

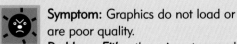 **Symptom:** Graphics do not load or are poor quality.
Problem: *Either* there is not enough memory available *or* you have the wrong display setting.
Solution: *Either* quit other applications (see Quick Fixes) *or* make sure that your monitor control is set to 640x480x256 or VGA.

 Symptom: There is no sound (PCs only).
Problem: Your sound card is not Soundblaster compatible.
Solution: Try to configure your sound settings to make them Soundblaster compatible (refer to your sound card manual for more details).

 Symptom: Your machine freezes.
Problem: There is not enough memory available.
Solution: *Either* quit other applications (see Quick Fixes) *or* increase your machine's RAM by adjusting the Virtual Memory.

 Symptom: Text does not fit neatly into boxes and "hot" copy does not bring up extra information.
Problem: Standard fonts on your computer have been moved or deleted.
Solution: Reinstall standard fonts. The PC version requires Arial; the Macintosh version requires Helvetica. See your computer manual for further information.

Index